What Do We Know Of Time?

poems by

Patricia Hemminger

Finishing Line Press
Georgetown, Kentucky

What Do We Know
Of Time?

Copyright © 2022 by Patricia Hemminger
ISBN 978-1-64662-988-6 First Edition
All rights reserved under International and Pan-American Copyright Conventions.
No part of this book may be reproduced in any manner whatsoever without written
permission from the publisher, except in the case of brief quotations embodied in
critical articles and reviews.

ACKNOWLEDGMENTS

Many thanks to the journals and websites in which versions of these poems
first appeared:

Streetlight Magazine "Out of Range"
The Blue Nib Literary Magazine: "What do we know of Time," "Mother's
Garden," "Rebirth" and "Returning Home to East Yorkshire."
Tiny Seed Literary Journal: "Why Ra Weeps"
River Heron Review: "Extinction Flight Path"
Twyckenham Notes: "The Owl" and "Ice Fishing"
Dragon Poet Review: "What I Fear Most," "Morning Walk," and "Debut."
The Ghazal Page: "Old Town Ghazal"
About Place Journal: "Going to the Farm in Winter"

Publisher: Leah Huete de Maines
Editor: Christen Kincaid
Cover Art: Gary Hemminger
Author Photo: Will Hemminger
Cover Design: John Hemminger

Order online: www.finishinglinepress.com
also available on amazon.com

Author inquiries and mail orders:
Finishing Line Press
PO Box 1626
Georgetown, Kentucky 40324
USA

Table of Contents

For Gary, Will and John
and my beautiful daughters-in-law, Alessandra and Lauren,
the grandchildren, Raef, Lars and Freya
and for my brother John for his encouragement

The Owl

One cold snap and the deer appeared in their winter coats,
grey like wolves. I would have hit them, huddled

by the roadside at dusk had it not been for their enormous eyes
that stared strangely, as if they knew me.

The angel was sitting on the cedar fence when I turned
into the driveway and spoke to me again of joy

and the power to choose, reminded me of the cherry tree
that bloomed the day you died and how the thrush exults

wildly, over and over, like church bells calling us
to Mass through the narrow lanes when we were children,

insisting that the beauty of a human life is equal
to the song of a bird and somehow I knew this was true.

Then I saw the angel was an owl, her enormous wings
so white and wide and eyes that stared into me

and I wanted to know what she saw but just as I turned to look
she lifted her wings, and drifted, silent as a star into the night.

My Mitochondrial Eves

"At Malton, fifty burials, comprising thirty eight inhumations…have been recovered."
    –Peter Halko, The Parisi: Britons and Romans in Eastern Yorkshire

Crouched in the grave, beneath
grass barrows, below the town
where I was born, Iron-Age women
speak to me still, like grey birds
with long beaks that preen
among the white blossoms
of the rowan tree, seed
the world with their song.

I remember how I laughed
and sang as they walked with me,
a child at ease in the wild
lanes brimming with weeds:
lady's mantle, buttercup and yarrow,
whose seeds they crushed and baked
with grains mashed into gruel.

In summer we wove cloth, bright blue
and yellow, after shutting up the sheep
in the fallow field. I close my eyes
and smile, remember that time,
and how I begged for a brooch I saw
years later displayed in the British Museum.
It lay next to the sword I had seen

hung on a long-haired man, its hilt
half-horn, studded with beads
of red glass that sparkled like jewels
in my dreaming. The mothers showed me
how to carve chalk statuettes
with swords strangely attached
to their tiny doll-like backs.

Old Town Ghazal

When I was four I walked with my mother once
a week past the chestnut trees to the old part of town.

Hand in hand we strolled by fields where mares grazed, their names
etched on brass plaques nailed to the gates in the old part of town.

A worn stone step on pavement's edge marked the stagecoach stop,
where horses' rumps once ran with sweat, in the old part of town.

My mother sang in the twelfth-century church, echoed the long-gone
monks clothed in cloaks and woolen hoods in the old part of town.

We stopped at aunt's thatched roof house. The sisters planted berry
bushes, wore wellington boots as they dug in the old part of town.

My grandmother rested in bed, white hair loose like spun wool,
her gentle face pressed against the pillows in the old part of town.

Mother dusted the walnut dresser, scrubbed the sink and black iron
stove. I wandered into the garden in the old part of town.

Do you remember, Patricia, the velvet petals, black and pink,
how tall the hollyhocks, how sweet the plums in the old part of town?

What I fear most

is smallness, not the mouse, or cockroach
that scurries across countertops at night,
dull exoskeleton clicking,
as sleepless again I reach for the light.

Not the ladybug or mayfly that lives
just one day to copulate, then falls,
wings extended to the water
to squeeze out eggs as she dies,

but small thoughts: the worry
of what you think, am I
smarter, are those wrinkles,
and where are you now?

I fear there will be no thoughts of stars
stretching back through time, of sea
shells on mountaintops, of strange
spiked fossils, extinct creatures,

like the last white-horned rhino
that died in the zoo
a few days ago, unseen
by our grandsons   forever.

Extinction Flight Path

Réunion kestrel, Falco duboisi—extinct (c.1700)
–New World Encyclopedia

Let go, let go the kestrel calls:
the chick drops from the nest's lip
wings shaking like dandelion clocks
pitched in the wind, trusting
like *Iberomesornis*, sparrow-sized
dinosaur testing bristle feathers for short
glides, that wind uplift works.

Come back, come back.
But it is too late: their soft bodies
refuse the ache of birth, abandon
bones in desert sand, overcome
escape velocity, spiral out
between the stars, great cosmic
sunflowers, that seed planets like ours.

Ice Fishing

Stretch marks ridge the lake's surface, molten ice
thickens like stained glass windows in the old church

where you married. Water puddles beneath the timber dock,
wood ducks huddle and groom, their yellow beaks sift

plumes, the way old women absentmindedly fluff
pillows on island terraces. Gone the flocks of white geese,

like bright snow lights flying south, gone
the crushed tangerine carpet that skirted the stripped maple.

Fish breathe in slow motion below the stiff winter sheet,
opaque as your still gentle face when you said, *please
don't feed me anymore.*

Two Worlds

Suppose the worries you entertain about the pain
in your back and the fact that your heart beats
unevenly sometimes and bad thoughts about friends
who forget to include you and the secret sense
that somehow you are better than they create
an imaginary world you live in as if it were real?

Meanwhile you miss the snow floating
onto rooftops, leaves that whisper
like children beneath the lavender bush,
the chatter of squirrels wearing
their fluffed tails like coats and the engine hum
of a car dawdling by early morning.

Morning Walk

Surf slowly washes sand, turns
it over and over, sifts pebbles from shells
ridged like bleached oriental fans.
A blue stone rolls, stops,
sparkles at our feet as we slip
like ghosts on the edge
of morning. "Is it a lozenge?"
you ask, your mind empty now
of neural networks spiraling out
like roots searching for water. Forget
falling through the hourglass, see
how the earth tilts, reflects
beauty in your wrinkled face
in waves that ripple across
shimmering sea.

New York Summer

Sweat drips down my back. I wait
for the bus on a slatted bench. An old man,
beard unkempt, tells of notarizing
his will. Two boys, five or six, in red
"We Are the Future" T-shirts skate
the sidewalk, swinging hockey sticks.
Nanny trails behind. I rise
to let a stooped woman sit.
"Thank you," she smiles and stares,
and in that moment my mind opens
to spaciousness, and I see that we
are mayflies of the cosmos—
alive this short uncertain time—
then suddenly her blue scarf shifts
in the wind and the thought:
"What would it be like not to have been born?"

Debut

For Will

Just as the turning world opens
to each fresh day, early
tulip leaves uncurled that spring,
hungry for sun's rays
to open their stomata, breathe in
their apportioned packet of sky.

When the weather warmed we sat
in the garden, waiting
for you to be born,
watched tulip's velvet soak up sun.

You must have sensed the tightening
in the womb, as poppy seeds sense
the lengthening light, reach up to astound
us with their red beauty, burst out,
as you did, eyes wide open, delighting
the nurses in their stiff blue dresses.

I Finally Wake Up Before Dawn

A friend encouraged me to write
a light poem, something silly when,
for instance, clumsy, I let
crumbs from my muffin
clutter the table,
pace the kitchen
create a mess before dawn,
walk out in the garden
in my black and frilly pajamas,
clutching coffee, Colombia Luminosa, dark roast
to wonder at the rising sun,
sit on the cedar bench, watch worms hide
as robin waits head bent on one side
listening with its non-ears,
each creature trying
to survive, as I am, pretending
to be wise instead of embracing
each unpredictable day, as it rambles—
like those curlicue brambles in my grandmother's garden—
still somehow avoiding that certain fact
that one day, like you, I will die
so that a hundred years from now
there will be no one
surviving who knew me
so why not lounge in the garden
in frilly pajamas.

Why Ra Weeps

Today, pollinators—especially Western honey bee populations—
are at a critical crossroads.
—Robert M. Nowierski, "Pollinators at a Crossroads" USDA
Blog June 24, 2020

Bee scouts dance, waggle and sway
point the way to scented patches:
peonies before the petals fall,
foxgloves bearded tongues,
which, shaded at wood's edge
call like monk's bells, summoning
the faithful to partake, savor
sacred bread, drink the wine.

Worker bees encode the flight
path into their striped bodies,
yellow and black like the mask of King Tutankhamun.
Bee wings flap and oscillate, generate
small hurricanes to uplift them.
The long proboscis siphons nectar,
food for gods, which bees store
in honey sacs, like chipmunks
store seeds to feed pups beneath the woodpile.

Just as Babylonian gods spit into clay
to create us, bees create seeds
to sustain us: with one swift stroke of their leg
yellow the sticky stigma with pollen
that tunnels to the soft ovary,
seeds the plants and fruit we eat,
apples, cranberries, melons, squash
cucumber, zucchini and black-eyed peas.

The tears of the Sun God fell
to Earth, became bees to honey the world

Going to the Farm in Winter

Past the stone walled field
littered with wild phlox in springtime,
past the church cemetery
and 1820 tavern home,
past the pheasant farm
red cap and mottled wings,
past the frozen stream
and water iced lawn,
past the hotel house
candles in every window,
past the country store with neon lights
red barns broken by age and weather,
past crows scratching at a frozen carcass,
deer with coats as thick as sled dogs,
a cart horse still and stolid in the frozen air.

Onions in bins, winter squash,
dirt caked carrots and celeriac,
crisp Chinese cabbage,
turnips and twisted parsnips,
hour-old eggs and homemade cheese.

Talk of gardens in the dead of winter,
a full moon and mist over the frozen lake,
fine snow gathering, a long way home.

Stork and Fox

Rain misted my eyes as I walked past the thatched roof
cottage at canal's edge, when Stork suddenly appeared, red

legs and beak, from behind hollyhocks where she'd stood,
on one leg of course, half asleep at dusk. She wanted,

she said, to warn me about Fox, who slinks from his hole
each sunset, hunting to feed his hungry cubs. I knew Fox

from an encounter last month when I met him running
from the chicken coop, an unfortunate hen in his jaws.

But I was glad to see Stork and wanted to ask why she stood
on one leg and what was the baby business all about,

but she only nodded rather formally then lifted her wings
and soared, long legs trailing, into the darkening sky.

It was then that I noticed beneath the hedgerow, small
red-tinged feathers trapped in the twigs of an empty nest.

Time to Move On

Roadside snowdrops clump.
Early morning sun blinds the eyes,
reflects off the canal. Two ducks
squat in a patched field

while birds, black and white,
like flying dice, swarm overhead, land
in mud stained stubble. Geese gather
in a tree's solid shadow, rise

together. Do they know where
they're going, remember
the cycle or do they just feel
the cool breeze feather

their beaks, dusk descend
too soon and know it's time
to move on? Above the horizon
a metal windmill turns.

Smoke

After Li-Young Lee

As a child I breathed in smoke from coal
hearths in each wall-papered room,
so a whiff conjures the narrow gas-lit
lanes, chameleon flames climbing in the grate.

Smoke seeped into my father's lungs,
stained them just as the charcoal sticks
we drew with in school dusted our fingers,
as he sat by the fire with his cigarette.

I did not know then that one day, breathless,
he would no longer climb the stairs
and I would sit with him, knowing
this was the last time, watching

his fine steady blue eyes—*The last gentleman*
our neighbor called him—
seeing him clearly, perhaps
for the first time.

He laughed and told me again
how he fished with his friends, rubber boots
up to their thighs, bamboo rods arced as they cast
their lines into rivers running with trout,

Sad moods and old harshness gone
like the cigarette smoke that drifted over green fields,
when as sweethearts he and my mother
sat on the grass, ate strawberries by the stream.

Night Fishing

Water, grey like tinted glass curls
out behind the boat. Lakeside windows
glow, expose dollhouse rooms like tableaux
in a TV show: a family round the table laughs,

a woman lingers by the window.
In a room with wooden beams a baby
hangs over the side of a highchair,
small hand reaching for a black dog.

The lambent August moon brushes
the horizon. We dock at the pier. Two boys
cast lines into the lake. "Catch anything?"
I ask. "Yes a two-foot bass and pickerel,"

one replies. His black eyes stare,
suspicious now, he feigns disdain,
shrugs and says, "We're supposed to throw
them in again." I walk away not looking back.

One by One

Many of the bright stars you see
may by now have exploded—
flung their elemental seeds,
like jewelweed's pressured pods
to birth new planets whirling
in the stellar sea— creating
black spaces, unseen by us, above.

It took a week for the letter
to arrive, saying my cousin
had died. It's not that we
were so close, he talked a lot,
mostly about himself, but now
there is only my brother and me.

Footprints

Some of the most distinctive intertidal finds are the human and animal footprints preserved in intertidal sediments….The earliest, at Happisburgh, are dated between 0.78 and 1 Ma
— *Bailey G. et al. (2020) Great Britain: The Intertidal and Underwater Archaeology of Britain's Submerged Landscapes.*

We sit on the deck, *thinking of nothing*
much. Summer day. Blue-green sky
smudges the horizon. We clink glasses,
welcome the black-capped, yellow-beaked terns

that crowd the shore companionably,
like a dazzle of zebras, dipping their heads
at a watering hole. We eat pizza: green

dots of chopped kale, black olives
and goat cheese, wispy strips of red onion.
A breeze blows off the retreating sea.

The children tumble onto the beach,
search for striated shells, starfish
to throw back. Barefoot we follow,

parents, grandparents, uncles and aunts,
leave footprints in the sand, just as
our long-armed ancestors did, seeking

shellfish and crab on mud-flats
where the Thames flowed into the sea,
a million years back.

The Sound of You Speaking to Me

Eardrums press in
as the plane descends:
the sound of being underwater.
I watch your mouth
form words, like a deaf woman
read your lips.

What makes a voice violent and shrill
like hemlock branches whipping
in the wind? Or soft, like dragonfly wings
at dusk? The way you lingered when we said goodbye:
mute as fog dissolving
on the pavement,
words unspoken.

Late Autumn

The boughs are thick
with beauty, crinkled
leaves yellow and red.

Each year, it seems,
the brittle brilliance
transcends the year before,
or perhaps as the days
shorten red intensifies
to scarlet, yellow vivifies
in gold, dazzling
despondency, loosening
its dark handhold.

Another World

For Gary

It was not a scent
but your voice that opened the door,
not only words but sounds, deep
like a stream whose turbulence
tells of its origin in the sea, its slow ripples
of the stretch of tangled weeds,
that revealed us, standing there
with nothing now between us.

Discovering Pascoli in Barga

Shutters close out the noon light, rattle
like branches before the storm. We lie together,
still in the coolness of the stone house,
tired from scaling hills to gather chestnuts,
climbing the Duomo's worn steps.
In the nave marble columns stand
on the backs of stone lions. One with claws,
sharp as scythes, clasps a dragon, the other crushes
a man, who caresses with one hand and stabs with the other.
After noon we wander the far hills, sit above the fog,
read Pascoli and hear *uneasy screeches of the lost*
birds in the skeletons of beeches.

What Do We Know of Time?

Without realizing it we had begun to feel
the scorching days, ninety degrees in our garden,
would never end.

The houseplants wilted. I set them out under the porch,
healing Aloe and Peace Lily, hosed them down
in the tarnished copper tray, remembering

a fish restaurant in Wellfleet last summer, pink
popsicles of allium, blue spiked delphiniums, lavender's
purple haze among corroded metal tabletops

where my husband amused himself squeezing
a lemon, watched as the black surface dissolved.
I poured vinegar onto the discolored planter and waited.

Small bright golden spots emerged, then coalesced
to shape what looked like Pangea, supercontinent
that held for one hundred million years.

What do we know of time? Stars survive
millions of years at the edge of spaciousness.
Small stars, our sun, blaze on for billions.

The world gains luster as it falls apart:
Our friend has been told they can do no more
for him, perhaps three months, maybe at most a year.

He is a physicist, aware of relativity, of the slowing
of time as gravity increases, how a moment
in the bright light of morning can expand into forever.

We sit with him in the sun, drink
tea and savor small bites of homemade
chocolate cake, crumbs scatter on the paper plates.

Gravity

Sadness is real I tell you,
the downturned mouth is not a caricature.
I can feel the weight that arcs
the lips, drags down the rest of the face,
heaviness in the chest that depresses.

The green countertops, shiny and slick,
black plastic chairs in the café sit
empty, where I came for company.

A child at the door peers in
to the past and I remember pressing
my nose to the glass of the sweetshop
window, where licorice was only
a penny a stick and I licked
lemon sherbet from a paper cup,
dawdling home on bright summer nights.

I smile at that memory,
reversing the downward pull.
Lightness lifts my chest
and in my mind I fly
like a hollow boned bird,
soar on velvet feathers.
Then the thought: could sadness
just be the body's response to gravity?

Imprints

The human hand forms one of the most ancient themes of human art…critical evaluation of existing data have shown that they are among the earliest examples of European Upper Palaeolithic cave art, stretching back at least to 35,000 (calendar) years ago.
  —A Research Project of the Department of Archeology, Durham University, UK

In the womb little hands
wave like mittens, webbed
fingers fused.

When did digits
separate, like bat bones
hidden under taut tissue,
curl out from webbed feet
to carve maps on mammoth tusks,
crimp clay pots, pick through
parched cereal grains,
string fox teeth, hammer green gold
into foil thin as skin?

Whose fingers grasped
horsehair brushes, combined
mined iron deposits
with spit or animal fat,
recreated surging bison
aurochs, spotted horses,
a man-bull sorcerer
along the calcite walls,
engraved the owl, head rotated
one hundred and eighty degrees
to look back at us?

Whose fingers separated
on rock, red ochre sprayed
proclaimed *I was here?*

Out of Range

Consider the pattern of UV light
directing bees to the flower's center.

Magnetic fields, unfelt by us
guiding geese in migration.

The low inaudible sounds
elephants hear with approaching kin.

That butterflies stand on a leaf
to taste with their feet.

Tiger moths ultrasonic clicks
jam bats' echolocation beams.

And snakes have holes in their faces
to detect their prey's infrared radiation.

I tell you again she is gone forever.
You answer not all things can be seen.

Return

For John

We drove to the country
so you and your brother
could ride tricycles outside,
play hide and seek among trees.
One weekend you suddenly asked,
"What happens when you die?"
I looked at your father, eyes wide.
"It's okay," you laughed, "I remember now."
You sounded smug
as only a four year old could.
"Your skin drops off, you're back
 to your bones and back to God."
Then you turned away
to play with your yellow truck.

Rebirth

All my childhood in the cuckoo's song,
frost-tinged grass at daybreak.
The sun marks a path across the stone
walk to the beech tree: young leaves
poke from old growth, uncurl
like a newborn's fingers.

Do not listen
to the doubts of old men.
The pear tree is heavy with white
blossoms that shift in the breeze like plumes
of a goose grooming itself
beside the canal.

The muscular flap of a swallow's wings
guides it to eaves of the brick house beyond
the garden: blue carpet of forget-me-nots,
daisies dress the grass like yellow buttons
on a baby's white jacket. From the doorway
I hear my mother calling.

Returning Home to North Yorkshire

I had forgotten the shape
of chestnut trees, deep green
hedgerows, crows on clay roofs,
stone walls dividing fields,
sheep scattered on the slopes.
.
I had forgotten the mosaic floor,
remnant of a Roman fort,
bordered with red and black
squares, deep pit excavated
beneath the orchard when I was four.

I had forgotten how I dawdled, plucked
daisies on grassy mounds,
one now found to house an Iron Age queen,
blue glass beads and chariot wheels
speed her to the afterlife.

We must all bury the dead.

Your gravestone looks fresh.
It must be the constant rain
that keeps the mottled marble clean.
I kneel to place pink heather
in its plastic pot. The florist said
it would last a long time.

Time Travel

I dreamed of you last night.
Medieval times. A falcon shrieked,
tents flapped red and gold.
We held hands in the dream,
had not seen each other for a long time.
A friend whispered,
"She is married now too."
You pushed me away gently
but we laughed because we knew
it was there, would always be there,
even though we cared
for others, had children now.
Then I woke and you brought me coffee
and I saw that it was still you.

The Spaces In Between

Roses are in bloom again, with all their redolent memories,
trellis flushed pink against blue delphiniums that crowd bright borders.

House sparrows splash in the stone birdbath, carved limestone bowl
on four grey columns, solid in creased photographs before I was born.

Of course we knew there would be suffering: late frost
kills the apple blossom, the hawk cracks the cuckoo's neck,

a gunshot or a last hospice breath ends a life and only then
do we understand meaning belongs to the feeling world

that lawmakers cannot bear to inhabit, do not dare to hear
the cries of a caged child separated from the mother, terrorized

by dreams—black robes fly like ravens in the moonless sky.
Yet in the spaces in between, in the rustling of leaves, in the garden

pulling weeds, in the kitchen chopping onions, in the faded
photographs, in the changing light at dusk life finds us.

The experience of growing up in rural North Yorkshire, UK along with her science background and love of nature informs and inspires **Patricia Hemminger**'s poetry. *Spillway, Parabola, Streetlight Magazine, The Blue Nib Literary Magazine, River Heron Review* and *Tiny Seed Literary Journal* among others have kindly published some of her poetry. Her poem, "Out of Range," earned an honorable mention in *Streetlight Magazine*'s 2020 Poetry Contest. Patricia is a science and environmental writer and associate editor of Pollution A to Z published by Macmillan. She is currently executive producer of a documentary focused on green chemistry solutions to environmental pollution. She holds a Ph.D. in chemistry and is a graduate of NYU's Science, Health and Environmental Reporting Program (SHERP) and of Drew University's MFA Poetry and Poetry in Translation Program. Patricia lives with her husband in Sussex County, New Jersey.

Lightning Source UK Ltd.
Milton Keynes UK
UKHW012102020123
414739UK00008B/103